Intermediate JAZZ CHORD VOICING

for Keyboard

by Bill Boyd

- The II-V-I chord voicings written out in all keys
- Practical experiences in comping and solo playing with a rhythm section
- Well over 100 examples to play and analyze

ISBN 0-7935-0056-7

HAL•LEONARD™
CORPORATION

7777 W. BLUEMOUND RD. P.O. BOX 13819 MILWAUKEE, WI 53213

FOREWORD

This book explores contemporary chord voicings and their applications to melody and accompaniment playing with a jazz group.

Some knowledge of chord construction is helpful in order to successfully proceed with this volume. As each new chord voicing is introduced, it is placed within the context of the II-V-I chord progression in several keys. The appendices contain this progression in all keys. The last two chapters include practical experiences in comping and melody playing.

The subject of chord voicing is so vast that it would be impossible to cover all the chord structures. Some of the more important voicings used by prominent jazz artists have been selected for inclusion in this book. There are over one hundred examples and exercises to play and analyze. Chapter assignments require experimentation with actual jazz tunes taken from sheet music or FAKE books. The careful preparation of each chapter will improve performance and provide a background for more advanced study.

CONTENTS

1: BASIC AND VARIATION CHORD VOICINGS

Detailed explanations of chord construction and of all the material discussed in this chapter are contained in AN INTRODUCTION TO JAZZ CHORD VOICING FOR KEYBOARD, the first book in this series. Also included are the Position 1 and Position 2 voicings for all chords and the II V I chord progression in all major and minor keys.

Seventh chords provide the basis for jazz harmony. Ninths, elevenths and thirteenths are added to the seventh chords. For additional color, the fifths, ninths and elevenths may be altered (raised or lowered one half step). Most altered notes appear in dominant seventh chords. COMBINATION CHORDS are dominant sevenths containing the ninth and one or more altered notes.

CHORD VOICING refers to the way in which the notes of the chord are distributed between the two hands.

BASIC VOICING
Position 1

The thumb of the right hand ALWAYS plays the third of the chord. The second finger plays the fifth, the third finger plays the seventh and the fifth finger the ninth. It is important to memorize which finger plays each chord member as this is the fingering for all types of chords both altered and unaltered in Position 1. The left hand plays the chord root.

Position 2

The right-hand thumb plays the seventh of the chord, the second finger the ninth, the third finger the third and the fifth finger plays the fifth. This fingering remains the same for all chords in Position 2. The left hand plays the chord root.

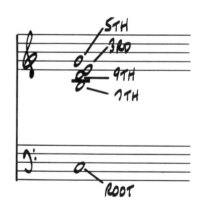

The thumb acts as a guide for the two positions. Position 1 may be referred to as "the position of the third" as the thumb is always on the third of the chord. Position 2 is the "position of the seventh" as the thumb is on the seventh of the chord. The one exception to this thumb rule is noted on the composite fingering and chord chart which appears at the conclusion of this chapter.

VARIATION VOICINGS

Position 1

The seventh of the chord is omitted from the right hand and added to the left hand seven steps above the root. All other fingerings remain the same.

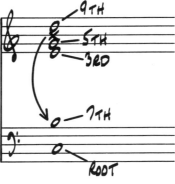

Position 2

The third of the chord is omitted from the right hand and added to the left hand three steps above the root. All other fingerings remain the same.

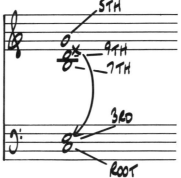

Chords are labeled by letter name and/or Roman numerals. These labels are called CHORD SYMBOLS. The letter name of the chord is the same as the root. The Roman numeral expresses the chord in the context of a key. In a major key the III chord is constructed on the THIRD step of the major scale. In the key of C major the III chord is an E chord.

Other labels identify the chord type or family (major, minor, etc.)

MAJOR	letter alone M7 MAJ. △7	Major triad Major 7th chord
minor	m - m7 min. 7 -7	Minor triad Minor 7th chord
DOMINANT 7th	7 (pronounced 7th)	Dominant 7th chord
DIMINISHED	0 or dim.	Diminished triad or Diminished 7th chord
HALF DIMINISHED	same as m7♭5	Half dim. 7th chord

Additional designations indicate notes which have been added to the chord.

$$C7^9 \quad CM7 \quad 6^9$$

The 5th and the 9th may be altered (raised or lowered one half a step). Altered notes usually appear in dominant seventh chords.

SYMBOLS FOR ALTERED CHORDS: ♭ or - = Flatted...lowered

or + = Augmented...sharp

$$C7^{\flat 9} \quad C7\#5$$

The 7th is sometimes not indicated in chord symbols where notes above the seventh are added to the chord. For example:

CM9 presumes the inclusion of the 7th (CM7^9)

C13 presumes the inclusion of the 7th and 9th (C7$^{9^{13}}$)

Note: The 6th and 13th are the same note and the flatted fifth and augmented 11th are the same note.

When one chord moves to another the movement is called a CHORD PROGRESSION. It is most practical to memorize chord voicings within the context of a progression. The II V I chord progression appears frequently in jazz tunes and is the basis for many of the examples in this book. In a major key the I chord is a major 7th, the II chord is a minor 7th and the V chord is dominant 7th altered or unaltered. In a minor key the I chord is a minor 6th or a minor 7th, the II chord is a minor 7th with a flatted 5th and the V chord is an altered dominant 7th.

When chord root movement is by half step, whole step or third, select the same chord voicing or position for each chord. When chord root movement is by fourths or fifths, alternate Position 1 and Position 2 voicings.

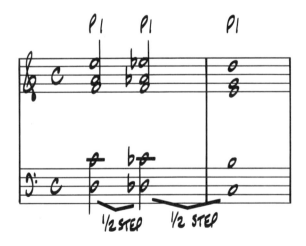

The following examples provide an overview of all the chord voicings in the introduction book along with a composite fingering chart for Positions 1 and 2.

Position 1   **Position 2**

Each chord is presented in Position 1 basic and variation voicing followed by Position 2 basic and variation voicing. All forms of the C chord serve as examples.

MAJOR

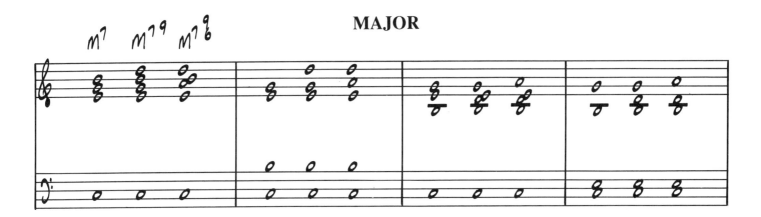

MINOR

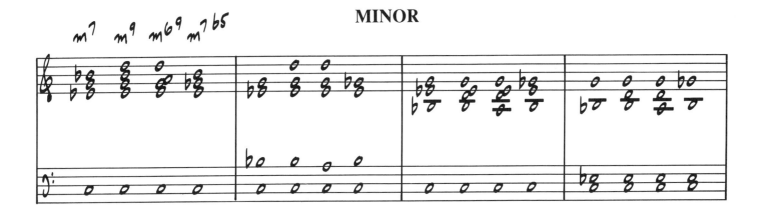

DOMINANT SEVENTH

DOMINANT SEVENTH ALTERED

DOMINANT SEVENTH ALTERED COMBINATION CHORDS

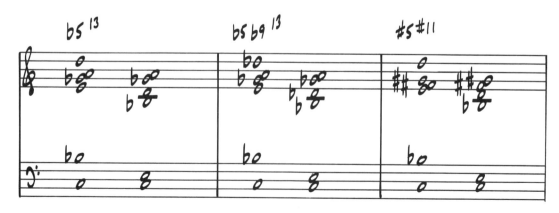

ADDITIONAL COMBINATION CHORDS AVAILABLE WITH VARIATION VOICING

2: ADDITIONAL I CHORD VOICINGS

The I chord in a major key may contain the sixth and ninth but not the seventh. In Position 1 the third finger of the right hand moves down from the seventh to the sixth. In Position 2 the thumb moves from the seventh down to the sixth.

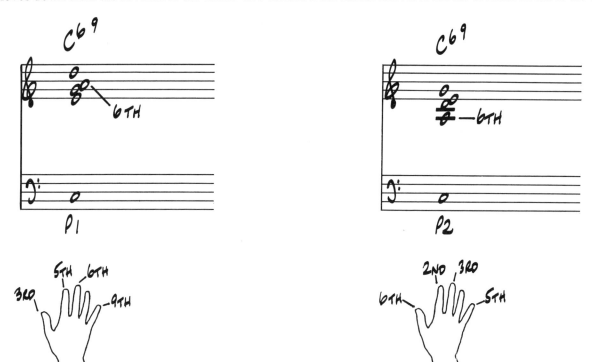

VARIATION VOICING

In Position 1 the fifth is omitted from the right hand and placed in the left hand five steps above the root. In Positon 2 the third is omitted from the right hand and placed in the left hand three steps above the root.

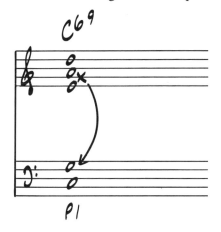

II   V   I:

10

The I chord in a minor key is usually minor sixth or minor seventh. The seventh may be raised one half a step. Inclusion of the ninth is optional.

Chord symbol: Cm#7   Cm#7⁹

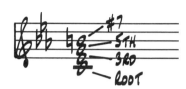
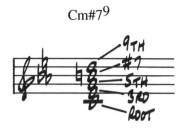

The most effective voicing is Position 1.

BASIC   **VARIATION**

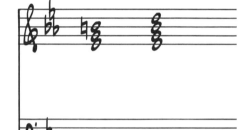
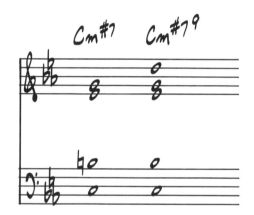

3: THE MINOR ELEVENTH CHORD

The eleventh note above the root may be added to the minor seventh chord.

In some instances, the fifth and/or the ninth are omitted from the voicing to avoid a cluttered sound.

BASIC VOICING

In Position 1 the 11th is played by the second finger and the fifth is omitted.

In Position 2 the 11th is played by the fourth finger and the 5th is omitted.

VARIATION VOICING

Position 1

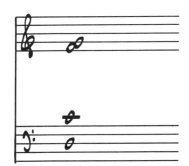

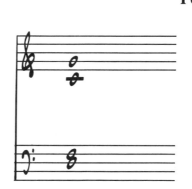

Position 2

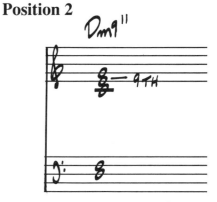

9th added

The most frequently used voicing for this chord places the 11th in the left hand instead of the 3rd. The 3rd is played in the right hand along with the 5th.

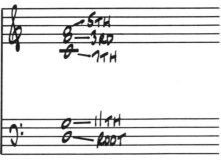

4: REVERSE VOICING

In more advanced comping situations it is necessary to abandon voicings with the root as the bottom note in order to not interfere with the bass player. The REVERSE voicing serves this purpose.

The notes in the basic voicing are played by the opposite hand. The root is played by the right hand and the notes formerly played by the right hand are played by the left hand. The notes assigned to each hand are the REVERSE of the basic voicing.

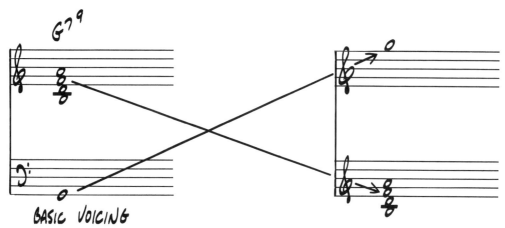

A further refinement deletes the 5th from the left hand and adds it to the right hand.

POSITION 1

Transfer the notes in the right-hand basic voicing to the left hand. Omit the 5th and add it to the right hand along with the root.

MAJOR

Select the 6^9 voicing instead of the $M7^9$.

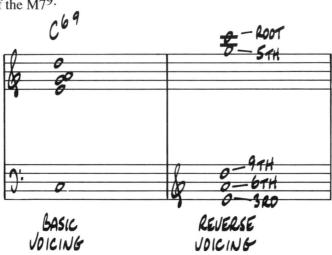

The REVERSE voicing sounds best in the middle of the keyboard. If played too low the sound is muddy. When played too high the sound is thin. Keep the notes within this range:

L.H. lowest note

R.H. highest note

The C6^9 voicing will sound better one octave lower.

In the right hand, the 7th may replace the root.

DOMINANT SEVENTH

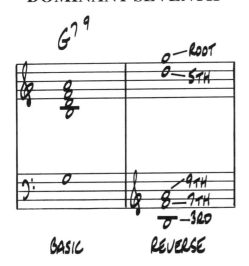

BASIC   REVERSE

13TH REPLACES
5TH

MINOR SEVENTH

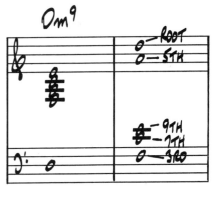

BASIC   REVERSE

POSITION 2

Transfer the notes in the right-hand basic voicing to the left hand and omit the 9th. The right hand plays the 9th and the 5th. There are no roots in the Position 2 voicings.

MAJOR

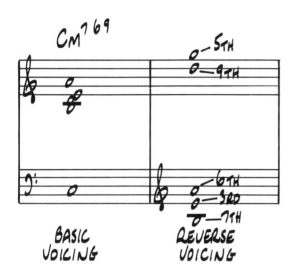

DOMINANT SEVENTH

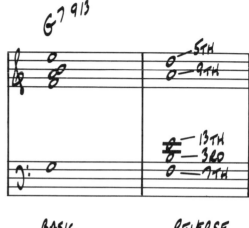

MINOR SEVENTH

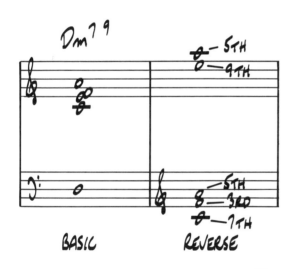

11th replaces 5th

Key of C MAJOR

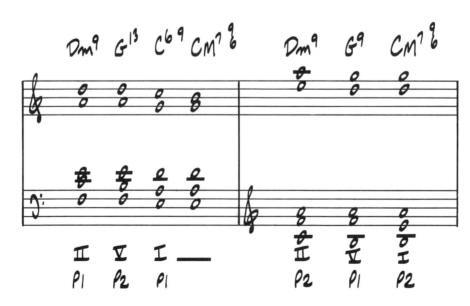

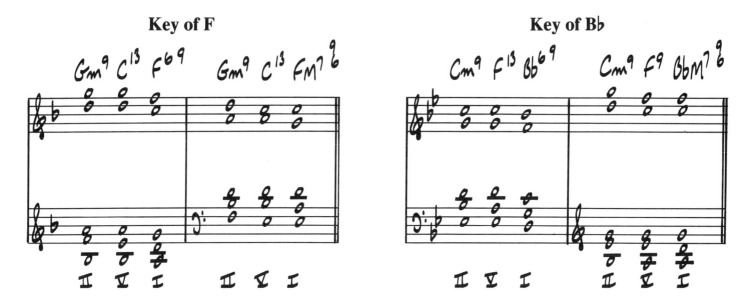

II V I REVERSE voicings for all major keys may be found in Appendix C.

ALTERNATE MINOR SEVENTH VOICING

In some chord progressions the inclusion of the 9th with the m7 chord is undesirable. A reverse voicing for another chord replaces the m9 chord. The Dm7^{11} and the F6^9 chords contain the same notes. Therefore the reverse voicing for the F6^9 may replace the Dm9 when the exclusion of the 9th is desirable.

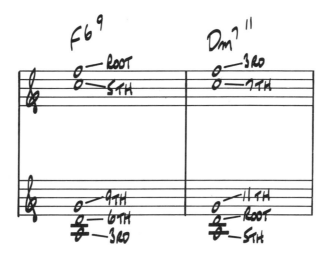

Obviously this relationship exists between any two chords whose roots are a minor third apart. Am11 equals C6^9...Gm^{11} equals B♭6^9 etc.

16

It helps to memorize the Reverse voicings by practicing the same position chords moving up or down chromatically. Play the following pattern and move down one half step each time. As you play, say the names of the chords.

Position 1

Position 2

ALTERED CHORDS

A few altered chords may be played with the Reverse voicing. A better voicing which is compatible with the Reverse voicing, will be presented in a later chapter.

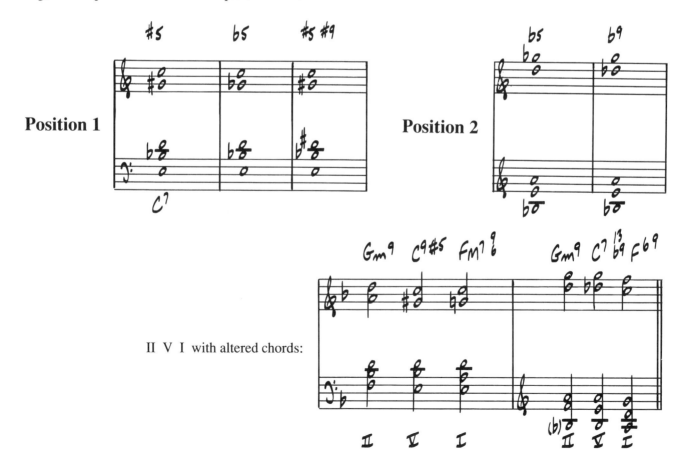

II V I with altered chords:

5: MINI VOICING

The essential chord tones may be played with as few as four notes...two in the left hand and two in the right. Thus the term MINI VOICING. The chord root is omitted. The 3rd and the 7th appear in the left hand and the 5th and 9th are in the right hand. This voicing is primarily for comping with a bass player. It is especially effective on electronic keyboards where other voicings may sound harsh or cluttered.

In Position 1, the 3rd and 7th are played by the left hand and the 9th and 5th are played by the right. In Position 2, the order in which the notes appear is reversed: L.H. 7th and 3rd...RH. 5th and 9th.

MAJOR

Position 1   Position 2

If the 6th, 7th and 9th are present, the 5th is replaced by the 6th in the right hand. With chords containing the 6th and 9th (but no 7th) the 7th is replaced by the 6th in the left hand in Position 1. Position 2 is an exception to the rule. The left hand plays the 6th and 9th and the right hand plays the 5th and the ROOT. There is no 3rd in this voicing!

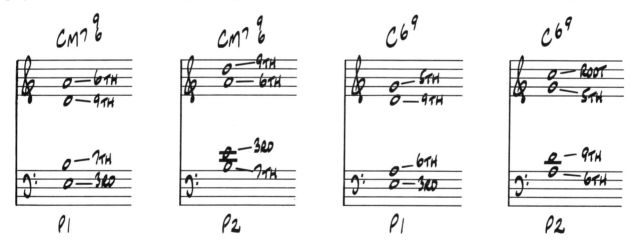

DOMINANT SEVENTH
The thirteenth chord omits the 5th from the right hand and replaces it with the 13th.

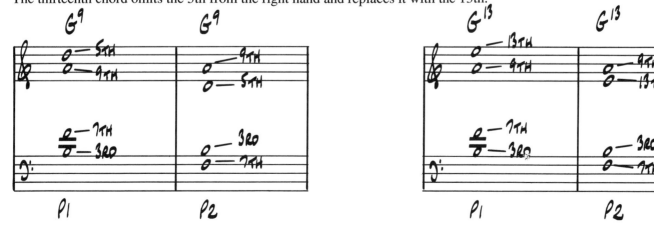

MINOR SEVENTH

In cases where the 9th must not be included in the m7 chord, follow the ALTERNATE MINOR 7th voicing principle set forth in Chapter 4, page 15. Apply the voicing for the 6⁹ chord whose root is a minor third above the root of the minor 7th chord. In this case the F6⁹ has the same notes as the Dm7 (11th).

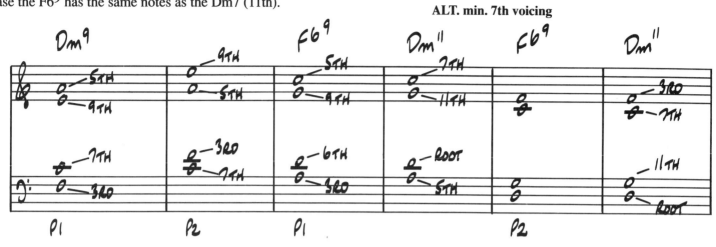

The II V I chord progression in the keys of C, F and B♭ major:

II V I MINI VOICINGS for all major keys may be found in Appendix D.

ALTERED CHORDS

All altered notes appear in the right hand. The G7 chord serves as an example for altered chords.

P. 1

P. 2

II V I chord progression with altered chords:

Play the following chord progressions several times. Each time alter the V chord with the various combinations of raised or lowered 5ths and 9ths.

6: CHORD SUPERIMPOSITION

When each hand plays a different chord simultaneously, the right-hand chord is said to be SUPERIMPOSED upon the left-hand chord. The notes played by the left hand are referred to as the FOUNDATION chord and serve as the basis for analyzing this dual chord structure.

In the above example, a D♭ major triad is superimposed upon a G major triad. The chord symbol is expressed in terms of the left-hand chord root. Chord superimposition is another type of chord voicing. There are many ways in which to superimpose one chord upon another. The most practical application is with major triads superimposed on dominant sevenths to produce altered chords. This method is compatible with all types of chord voicings but is particularly useful in conjunction with the Reverse voicing.

There are five major triads which may be superimposed on any given dominant seventh chord. Any inversion of the major triad may be played in the right hand. In Position 1 the left hand plays the 3rd and 7th of the foundation chord. In Position 2 the left hand plays the 7th and 3rd.

The C7 chord serves to illustrate the superimposed structure. The five major triads which compliment the C7 chord are D, E♭, G♭, A♭ and A.

Keep the hands close together. Do not overlap notes from one hand to the other.

II V I with superimposed V7 chords and Reverse voicing for the I and II chords in the key of F Major:

At this point perhaps a comment should be made regarding the fact that with the Reverse voicing there are three notes in the left hand and two notes in the right. When the superimposed voicing appears, there are two notes in the left hand and three in the right. Most keyboard music would be notated with the same number of notes in each hand. There are valid reasons for this unusual notation.

When practicing the various voicings, one develops a feeling in the hands. The Variation voicing "feels" a certain way which is completely different from the "feeling" of the superimposed or Reversed voicing. Part of the memory and playing process involves the conscious awareness of the way a particular voicing "feels" to the hands. In this instance, it is important to have a sense of moving from one type of voicing to another.

Secondly, the Reverse voicing will be applied to another style of keyboard playing in a later chapter. The development of this awareness of how the Reverse voicing feels to the hands will be helpful at that time.

SUSPENDED DOMINANT SEVENTH CHORDS

A suspended dominant seventh is a chord in which the fourth note above the root (11th) appears IN PLACE OF THE THIRD. The 4th and the 11th are the same note.

CHORD SYMBOL: C9 sus 4 or C11

This chord should not be confused with the augmented eleventh (flatted fifth) chords. The augmented 11th chord does include the 3rd.

A superimposed chord voicing is applied to this chord structure. For a C11 play a B♭ triad (any inversion) with the right hand and the root and the fifth in the left hand. The usual 3rd and 7th notes in the left hand are not necessary because there is no 3rd in the 11th chord and the 7th appears in the superimposed triad.

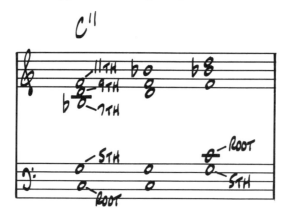

Sometimes the 5th is played below the root as in the last example above.

The following chart contains all of the dominant seventh chords followed by the major triads which may be superimposed on each. The 3rd and the 7th of the foundation chord are played in the left hand except in the case of the 11th chord which requires the root and the 5th of the foundation chord.

FOUNDATION CHORD	SUPERIMPOSED MAJOR TRIAD					
	13 # 11	#9	$\flat 5\flat 9$	#5#9	13$\flat$9	sus 4 (11)
C7	D	E$\flat$	G$\flat$	A$\flat$	A	B$\flat$
D$\flat$7	E$\flat$	E	G	A	B$\flat$	B
D7	E	F	A$\flat$	B$\flat$	B	C
E$\flat$7	F	G$\flat$	A	B	C	D$\flat$
E7	F#	G	B$\flat$	C	C#	D
F7	G	A$\flat$	B	D$\flat$	D	E$\flat$
G$\flat$7	A$\flat$	A	C	D	E$\flat$	E
G7	A	B$\flat$	D$\flat$	E$\flat$	E	F
A$\flat$7	B$\flat$	B	D	E	F	G$\flat$
A7	B	C	E$\flat$	F	F#	G
B$\flat$7	C	D$\flat$	E	G$\flat$	G	A$\flat$
B7	C#	D	F	G	A$\flat$	A

Follow the chart and practice the altered dominant seventh chords and the suspended chords in all keys.

7: DIMINISHED SEVENTH CHORDS

There are three different diminished seventh chords each containing four notes.

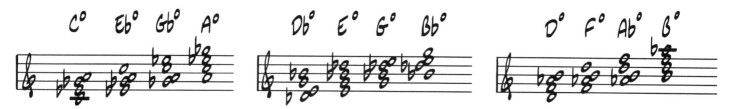

Any chord member may appear in the left hand as the root and any inversion may be played in the right hand.

A more contemporary sound is achieved by replacing the top note in any inversion with the note one whole step above. The added note may never be used as the root.

A better four note voicing for the contemporary diminished seventh chord places the root on the bottom and moves the 3rd to the top of the voicing.

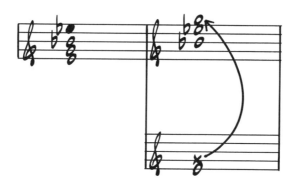

All the contemporary diminished 7th voicings appear below.

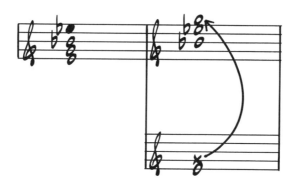

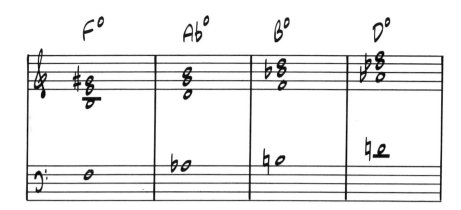

DIMINISHED SEVENTH CHORD SUPERIMPOSITION

Diminished 7th chords may be superimposed upon dominant 7th chords. Select the diminished 7th chord whose root is the same note as the 3rd of the dominant 7th chord.

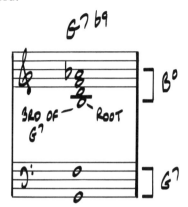

All inversions of the diminished 7th chord are acceptable.

When the inversions of the contemporary diminished 7th chord are superimposed upon the dominant 7th chord and are analyzed in terms of the foundation chord, they produce many altered notes.

The examples are the V chords in the keys of C, F and B♭ major.

8: II V I IN MINOR

The minor tonality is quite different from major and requires some special attention. The II V I chord progression in all minor keys with the Basic voicing, appears in the first book in this series. This chapter will address the Reverse and Superimposed voicings in the minor mode.

THE II CHORD

The II chord is a minor seventh with a flatted fifth. This chord is sometimes analyzed as a half diminished seventh chord. (symbol: $\emptyset$) The ninth may NOT be included in this chord but the eleventh is often present. In order to understand the Reverse voicing for the II chord, it is necessary to further analyze this chord structure.

The m7♭5 is three different chords:

The Reverse voicing for the II chord is based upon the Fm6. In the following example, the original Fm7 voicing serves as a model. In Position 1 the left-hand middle note moves from the 7th to the 6th. In Position 2 the left-hand bottom note moves from the 7th to the 6th.

Position 1

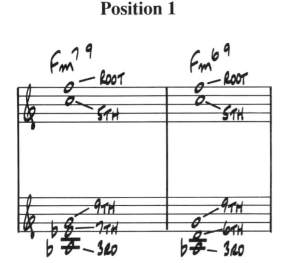

Position 2

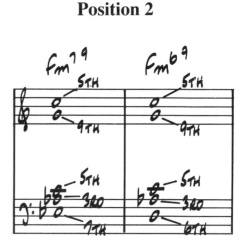

When the Fm6^9 chord is analyzed as a Dm7♭5, Position 1 has the ♭5 as the bottom note and the 3rd as the top note. In Position 2 the root is the bottom note. The 11th appears in the left hand in Position 1 and in the right hand in Position 2.

Position 1	Position 2

The voicing for the II chord in minor is an exception to the Reverse voicing rule for the left hand. The ♭5 is the lowest note instead of the 3rd in Position 1. In Position 2 the root is the lowest note instead of the 7th.

All m7♭5 Reverse voicings are based on the m6th chord whose root is a minor third above the II chord.

THE V CHORD

The V7 chord may not contain the 9th, 11th or 13th. The 5th may be altered (raised or lowered) but the 9th and 11th MUST be altered.

The Superimposed chord voicing is good for the V chord in a minor key when used in conjunction with the Reverse voicing. There are five major triads which may be superimposed upon the V7 foundation chord. Do not select one which contains the unaltered 9th, 11th or 13th.

13 #11	#9	♭5 ♭9	#5 #9	♭9 13
A	B♭	D♭	E♭	E
NO	GOOD	GOOD	GOOD	NO
G7	G7	G7	G7	G7

THE I CHORD

The I chord in minor is m6^9, m#7^9 and less frequently m7.

The m6^9 chord:

    In Positions 1 and 2 the 7th in the left hand moves to the 6th.

Position 1

Position 2

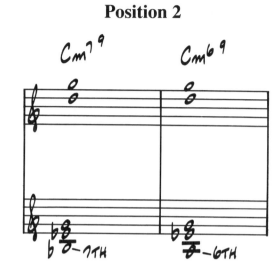

The m#7^9 chord:

    In Position 1 the root in the right hand moves down to the #7. In Position 2 the 7th in the left hand moves up to the #7.

Position 1

Position 2

II V I Key of Cm

9: STRETCH VOICINGS

Labels such as VARIATION, REVERSE and MINI are convenient terms in which to describe some of the chord voicings included in this book. STRETCH voicing is another such convenience label to describe a voicing which is a variation of Position 1 for minor and dominant seventh chords. The third is the bottom note of the right hand but in order to play all of the chord members, the hand must "stretch" the distance of nine steps.

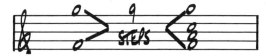

MINOR SEVENTH CHORDS

There are two versions of this voicing. They are interchangeable. Two choices are available because in some keys one might be too difficult to reach. The left hand may contain the root alone, the root and fifth or the root and seventh. The root and seventh sound best in the middle register and the root and fifth are best for the low register.

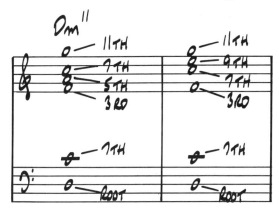

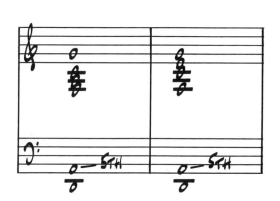

DOMINANT SEVENTH CHORDS

This is a #11 (b5) voicing with or without the 13th.

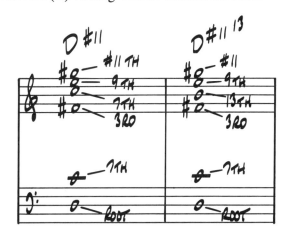

II V I Stretch voicings may be found in all major keys in Appendix E.

30

The following examples illustrate the stretch voicing in several keys. The A♭m11 chord does not contain the 9th as it would be difficult to reach.

Another voicing for Maj7, m7 and dominant 7th chords is also a variation of Position 1 and requires the right hand to stretch an octave. No altered notes or notes beyond the 7th appear in this voicing.

Play the original Position 1 basic voicing. Delete the 5th from the right hand and place it in the left hand above the root. In the right hand repeat the third one octave higher.

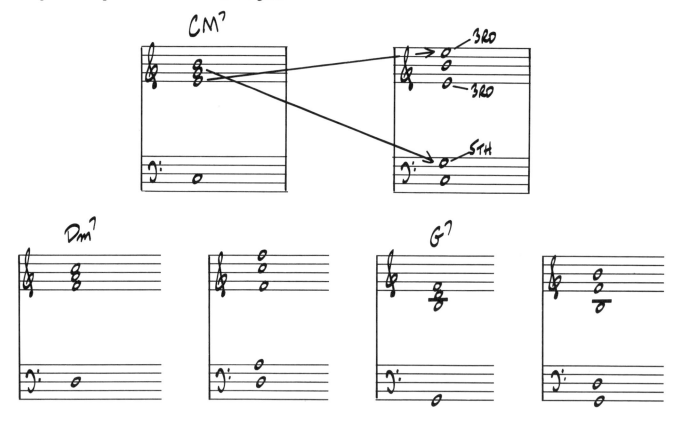

Combining the two types of Stretch voicings:

Position 1 and Position 2 voicings are alternated to avoid wide skips when chord roots move by 4th or 5th. Because this is only a Position 1 voicing, it is selected when chords move by whole step, half step or by third.

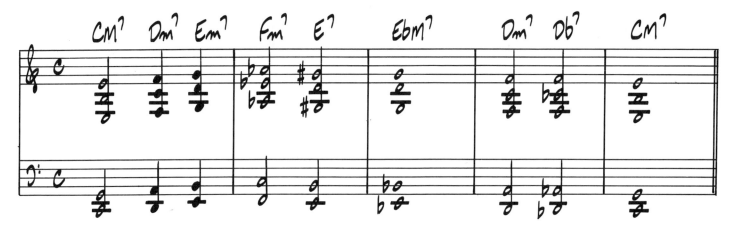

The example below combines this voicing with Position 2 variation voicings.

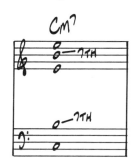

A variation doubles the 7th in the Left Hand:

The examples below are presented as "food for thought." Further development for solo playing will be presented in a future volume.

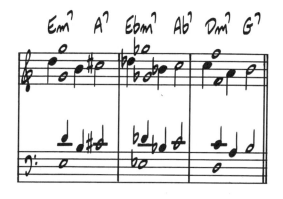

10: COMPING

COMPING is the jazz vernacular for accompanying. The keyboard player must be able to organize the many chord voicings into an accompaniment for jazz soloists, small groups or big bands. A review of the "COMPING" chapter in AN INTRODUCTION TO JAZZ CHORD VOICING is helpful before beginning this chapter.

SELECTING THE CHORDS FOR THE ACCOMPANIMENT

It is best to practice from a FAKE book. This type of book contains hundreds of melodies written on one staff with the chord symbols above. Fake books do not always indicate four note chords or chords with added and/or altered notes. Therefore these additions must be made in order to achieve a full and idiomatic jazz sound. Major and minor triads become major seventh and minor seventh chords with or without added notes. Augmented triads may be played as dominant 7th chords with the raised 5th. Dominant 7th chords may include added and altered notes when appropriate.

Some chords in a progression may be replaced with other chords. These "replacements" are referred to as SUBSTITUTE chords. The possibilities for chord substitution are vast. One of the most common is the tri-tone substitution.

The distance between two tones which are three whole steps apart, is an AUGMENTED FOURTH. This distance is sometimes referred to as a TRI-TONE.

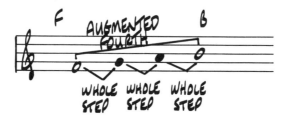

Any two dominant seventh chords whose roots are an augmented fourth apart will substitute for one another. The example above illustrates that F7 will substitute for B7 and B7 will substitute for F7. The dominant 7th chord may be altered or unaltered.

Ex.1

Ex.2

The notes in the B7 chord are written enharmonically to show they are the same as the notes in the F7 chord. For example, the G natural in example 1 is a sharp 5th in the B7 chord and normally would be notated as an F double sharp.

There are six augmented-fourth combinations. The dominant 7th chords built on these roots will substitute for one another.

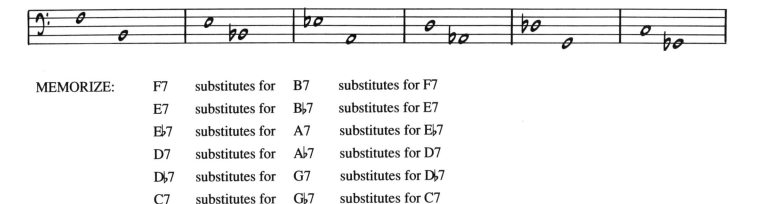

MEMORIZE:

F7	substitutes for	B7	substitutes for F7
E7	substitutes for	B♭7	substitutes for E7
E♭7	substitutes for	A7	substitutes for E♭7
D7	substitutes for	A♭7	substitutes for D7
D♭7	substitutes for	G7	substitutes for D♭7
C7	substitutes for	G♭7	substitutes for C7

The melody should be considered when selecting a substitute chord. If the new chord clashes with the melodic line then another alternative is necessary.

The six augmented-fourth substitutions are illustrated below. The right-hand notes are the same for both chords, only the roots change.

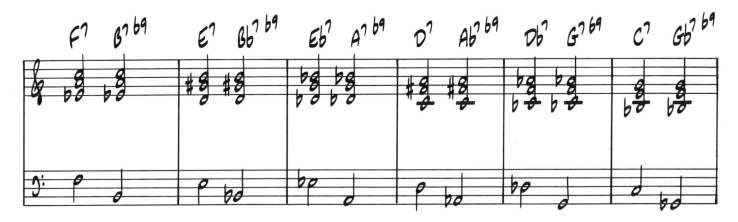

Accompaniments fall into two categories: those with a bass line and those without. A bass line may be provided in the absence of a bass player.

COMPING WITHOUT A BASS PLAYER

The Basic voicing has the essential chord tones in the right hand and the left hand is free to play a bass line. Bass lines consist of roots, fifths, chord tones and scale passages.

ROOTS AND FIFTHS　　　　　　**SCALE LINE**　　　　**CHORD TONES**

Roots may be approached from a half step above.

Select a song from the FAKE book. Study the chord progression, choose a chord voicing and memorize the chord progression without a bass line.

Basic Voicing:

Add a bass line.

Add rhythmic figures to the right hand. The figures should be uncomplicated and must compliment the soloist or group.

If a drummer is available the bass line is optional. In this case, select the Variation Voicing where the root is the bottom note.

Variation Voicing:

Notice that the left hand doubles the rhythm of the right hand.

COMPING WITH A BASS PLAYER

The bass player will provide the root movement. Therefore select voicings in which the root is not the bottom note. The Reverse and Superimposed voicings work well together in this situation. The Mini voicing is another alternative, especially with electronic keyboards.

Before proceeding, some attention must be drawn to the top notes in all of the chord voicings. When moving from one chord to another, these top notes form a melodic line of sorts. Choose chord positions which will allow the top notes to move by step, half step or by thirds. This will ensure smooth movement from one chord to another. This consideration should serve as a guide but some situations will dictate other top voice movement.

The following is a sixteen measure chord progression to a standard tune which is often played by jazz groups. The slashes replace the melody and represent the beats.

The first example illustrates the Reverse voicing. First, select the voicings and memorize them. Two notes in the left hand denote the Superimposed voicing.

36

Add rhythmic figures:

The following examples provide other voicing solutions to this chord progression. Play through the examples as written and then add rhythmic figures. Occasionally tritone substitutions appear.

Mini voicing:

Stretch voicings:

Variation voicing:

The next example shows the Basic voicing with a bass line. Practice the example as written and then add rhythmic figures to the right hand. Obviously this style would not be used when a bass player is present.

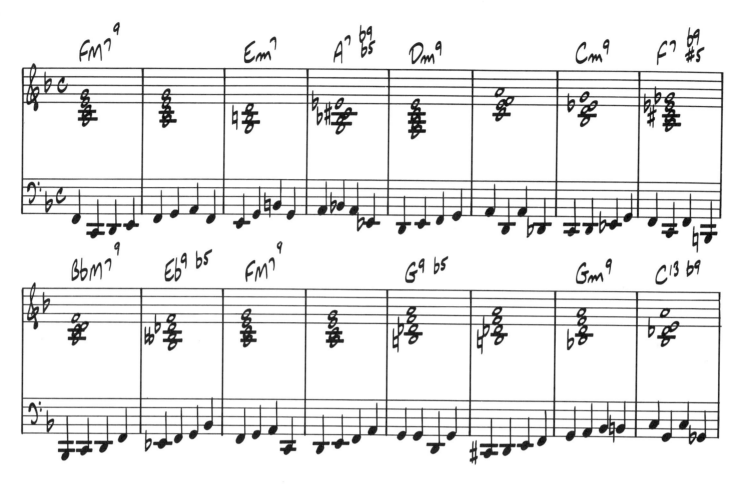

It is possible to link several different voicings together. The voicing selection and position must allow smooth (playable) movement from one chord to the other. Attention to the top note guidelines will help to insure smooth connections between voicings.

Key for analysation: R = Reverse   ST = Stretch   V = Variation   SP = Superimposed

Occasionally the top note in a voicing may be changed in order to create a better melodic line. The following is an example of the basic twelve-measure blues chord progression. The harmonization is with the Reverse voicing with some top note changes (marked *).

The twelve-measure blues chord progression with the Mini voicing follows. Sometimes chords move up one half step and back to the original chord. Examples of this appear in measures one, three and seven.

Chords with the top note changed.

Select jazz tunes from sheet music or a FAKE book and memorize the chord progressions. Develop accompaniments using several voicings. Practice alone and with a rhythm section and soloists.

The appendices in AN INTRODUCTION TO JAZZ CHORD VOICING and this book together contain most of the chord voicings in all keys.

11: MELODY PLAYING WITH THE RHYTHM SECTION

All voicings may be adapted to melody playing. It would be helpful to review the chapter on this subject in AN INTRODUCTION TO JAZZ CHORD VOICING.

VARIATION VOICING

An octave of potential melody notes may be reached in both Positions 1 and 2.

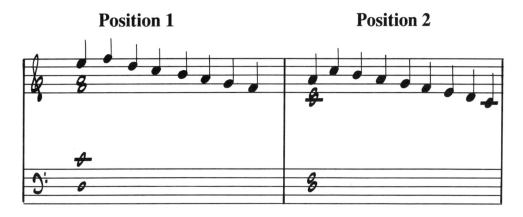

The following represents the first five measures of a melody as it might appear in a fake book.

STEP 1: Select a chord position which allows the melody to be played at the top of the voicing while the remaining chord members are sustained. Added notes, altered notes and substitute dominant seventh chords should be included. Memorize the chord progression.

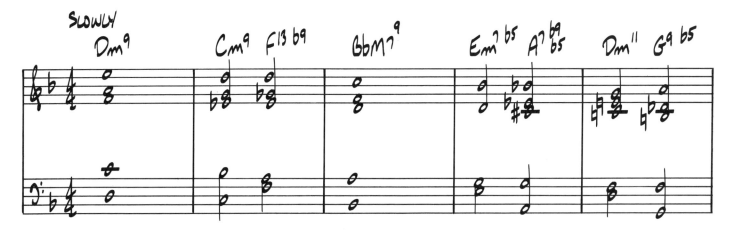

42

STEP 2: Play the melody as the top note of the voicing while sustaining the other chord members.

SLOWLY

Melody "B" is faster and more rhythmic.

MELODY "B"

STEP 1:

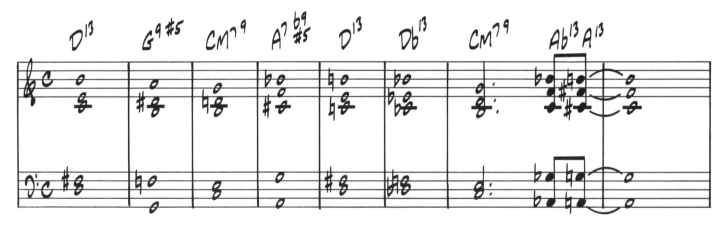

STEP 2:

BASIC VOICING

Another style of melody playing is especially effective with the rhythm section. The root movement is provided by the bass player. The right hand plays the melody one octave higher than written. The left hand plays the chord tones which were formerly played by the right hand in the Basic voicing.

STEP 1: Select the chord voicing and memorize the progression.

MELODY "A"

STEP 2: Transfer the notes from the right hand to the left hand.

STEP 3: Add the melody in the right hand one octave higher than written.

44

The last example began with a Position 2 voicing. In many instances it is possible to begin with either position. In this case, to start with Position 1 and continue causes the left hand to go too low and produce a muddy sound. Range is always an important consideration when selecting a position.

REVERSE VOICING

The Reverse voicing is one of the best voicings to select for melody playing with a rhythm section. The left-hand part of the voicing is played as an accompaniment while the right hand plays the melody or a jazz line. When the Reverse voicing is selected for comping, it is easy to switch to melody as the left-hand part remains the same.

The I chord voicing in Position 2 is based on the 6^9 Basic voicing instead of the $M7^6$.

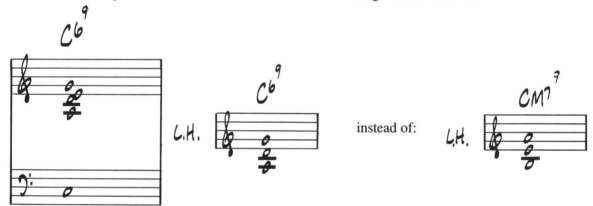

There are three choices for dominant seventh chords in both positions. Play the altered version, the unaltered version or the 3rd and 7th.

POSITION 1 **POSITION 2**

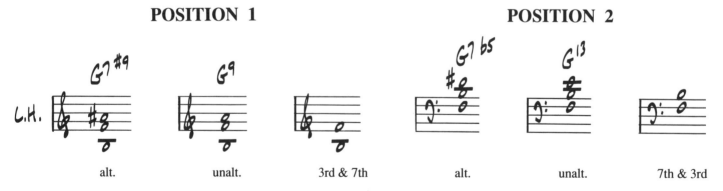

The selection depends on how well the voicing complements the melodic line.

Melody "A" with the Reverse voicing in the left hand.

Melody "A" with chord tones added to the right hand:

For more rhythmic songs, another style for melody voicing is effective. The right hand plays the melody in octaves, one octave higher than written. The left hand doubles the rhythm of the melody with the Reverse voicing.

MELODY "B"

A variation on this style places the melody one octave higher than written. One chord tone is added below the melody note. The left hand remains the same. Notes played by the left hand may be doubled in the right hand.

MELODY "B"

Since the Reverse voicing is effective for melody playing, it is important to memorize the left hand for IIm7 V7 I in all keys. (See the left-hand part in Appendix C. Adjust the I chord in P. 2.)

Another common jazz chord progression is I VI7 II7 V7 I. The left-hand Reverse voicings for this progression appear in Appendix F. The following example illustrates some left-hand Reverse voicing combinations for this chord progression.

These voicings contain no root. Because of the TRI-TONE substitution principle, all dominant 7th chords are two chords in one. The bass player may provide either root.

The following exercises apply the I VI7 II7 V7 chord voicings to a jazz line. Notice that occasionally the left hand emphasizes a rhythmic figure played by the right hand.

The same jazz phrase with different left-hand voicing combinations:

The following examples are jazz phrases in the key of C minor. The II V I left-hand Reverse voicings for all minor keys appear in Appendix G.

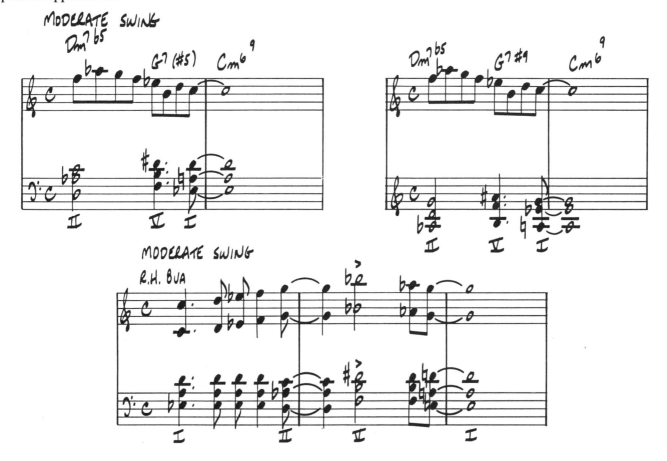

The twelve-measure blues chord progression with the Reverse voicing in the left hand and an improvised jazz line in the right hand:

Choose a song from the FAKE book. Apply some of the melodic devices described in this chapter. The nature of the melodic line will determine the approach to melodic voicing. Other factors include style and tempo. Octaves in the right hand will be difficult to play if the melody moves in fast eight notes or contains wide skips. The single-note style fits all types of melodies.

The material in this chapter by no means covers all of the possibilities for melodic voicing. Practice and listening to recordings of keyboard artists will eventually lead to acceptable solo playing.

APPENDIX A

VARIATION VOICING: IIm9   V13♭9   IM9

All Major Keys

APPENDIX A (Continued)

VARIATION VOICING: IIm9 V9$^{\#5}$ IM9

All Major Keys

APPENDIX A (Continued)

VARIATION VOICING: Alternate V7 Voicing   Symbol: ♭5♭913

Place these V7 chord voicings in the II V I chord progression in Appendix A.

APPENDIX B

BASIC AND VARIATION VOICING: Major add 6th and 9th   **Symbol: 6^9**

APPENDIX B (Continued)

Minor add #7 and 9th

Symbol: m#7⁹

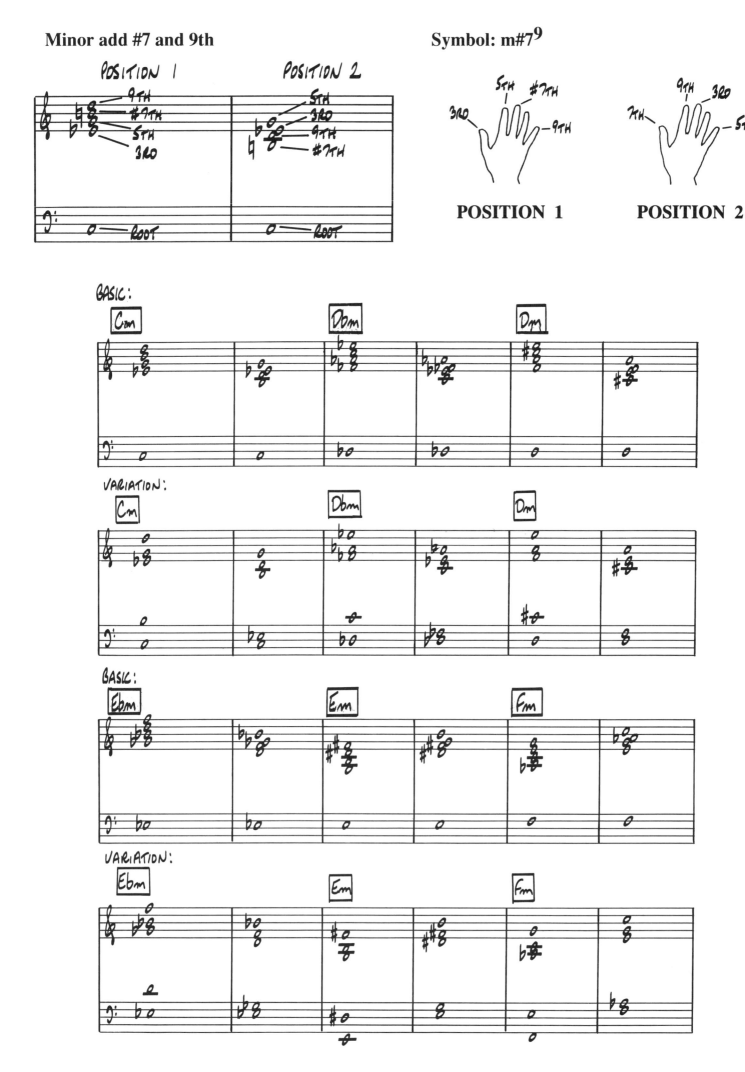

APPENDIX B (Continued)

56

APPENDIX C
REVERSE VOICING: II V I
All Major Keys

APPENDIX C (Continued)

All Major Keys

APPENDIX D

MINI VOICING: II V I (with altered V chord)

All Major Keys

APPENDIX D (Continued)

All Major Keys

APPENDIX E

STRETCH VOICING: IIm11   ♭II#11^{13} IMAJ7
All Major Keys

This is a II V I chord progression with the ♭II #11^{13} substituted for the V7 chord.

APPENDIX F

LEFT-HAND VOICINGS FOR RIGHT-HAND MELODY OR JAZZ LINES

I   VI7   II7   V7   I

APPENDIX F (Continued)

APPENDIX G

LEFT-HAND VOICINGS FOR RIGHT-HAND MELODY OR JAZZ LINES

II   V   I   Minor Keys